KITCHEN STUDIO PRESENTS THE INDIAN SPICES AND MASALAS

LET THE MAGIC BEGIN

INDIRA TALASILA

Copyright © Indira Talasila
All Rights Reserved.

This book has been published with all efforts taken to make the material error-free after the consent of the author. However, the author and the publisher do not assume and hereby disclaim any liability to any party for any loss, damage, or disruption caused by errors or omissions, whether such errors or omissions result from negligence, accident, or any other cause.

While every effort has been made to avoid any mistake or omission, this publication is being sold on the condition and understanding that neither the author nor the publishers or printers would be liable in any manner to any person by reason of any mistake or omission in this publication or for any action taken or omitted to be taken or advice rendered or accepted on the basis of this work. For any defect in printing or binding the publishers will be liable only to replace the defective copy by another copy of this work then available.

Author's Note

Hello! Reader,

As promised before Kitchen Studio came up with another topic (Indian Spices and Masalas) which is very favourite to you all." ***Its time for the masala magic to bigen***"

Worried about the same old taste of your food? Feeling bored to prepare the same food always. Be ready to learn some magic while preparing food for your family, friends, Relatives, and parties. Learn how to blend the spices and add magic to the dishes of your very own taste.

I was born in Andhra Pradesh's coastal area (East Godavari district Kakinada) and later moved to Maharastra where completed my Graduation in(Microbiology and Biochemistry)Even though I spent so much time in Maharashtra (Nagpur), my interest or taste for Indian food didn't change.I didn't realize when I fell in love with cooking and started experimenting with different variety of spices, but what I realized is after doing so much research my love for different cuisines has increased. I feel somewhere very strongly connected to my roots. All this has inspired me to write this book for true food lovers. People usually think it is very hard to prepare masalas at home because they require lots of hardwork, preparation, and are time-consuming. But I would proudly say they are very easy to prepare and the only thing is knowing the correct procedure, which you will be able to do by following the instructions in this book. I have focused only on the preparation of masalas and what all grocery [ingredients] you would require to prepare. Hope that, like me, you can discover many new blends and tastes during the journey.

Do explore, just don't forget to have fun when doing so.This is my second book on Indian food just a starting, there are several more to come, which I will include in my forthcoming editions, along with simple preparation strategies and tips.

I welcome any questions, comments, and opinions.

You can reach out to me at *indirat27@gmail.com*.

Contents

Grocery Store

Things needed to prepare masalas in this book

- Heavy bottomed kadai, /wide mouth pan
- spatula
- mixie big/ small jar
- plates
- cummin seeds
- cardomonn seeds
- coriander seeds
- mustard seeds
- methi seeds
- Jeera
- Badi Elaichi
- Dry Red chillies
- salt
- turmeric
- mint leaves/ Drt mint powder
- Fennel seeds(saunf)
- Star rinse
- Nut meg
- Mango powder
- Cinnamon sticks (dal chini)
- **pulses:**
- **Chana dal**
- **urad dal**
- **Roasted chana dal**
- Black pepper
- Cloves
- Shah jeera

- Garlic pods
- Bay leaves
- Asafoetida
- Mace
- curry leaves
- Garlic

Table Of Contents

1. Various types of Indian Spices, Benefits, and uses
2. Preparing different types of masalas in your very own kitchen.

- Dhania powder masala
- chat Masala Powder
- Rasam Powder
- Red Chilli Powder For Regular Use
- Garam masala powder
- Sambar Powder
- Gun powder podi
- Bonus Recipe (Shahi Garam Masala Powder)

3. Important tips to follow while preparing and storing the spices and masalas.

CHAPTER I

Different types of spices used in India.

Introduction:

Indian food is different from rest of the world, India is very rich in cultural heritage which makes it stand unique to other countries, having different climatic conditions in different parts of India, India produces many different varieties of spices.

Indian food is different with rest of the world not only with the taste but also the cooking methods it reflects a perfect blend of cultures and ages. Just like Indian culture, food of India is know for its taste and spiceness. Throughout India it may be north India or south India spices are perfectly blended and prepared to get that authentic flavour to the dishes. This perfectly using the ingredients and blending them makes the food deliciously tasty and unique. Indian spices have high health and medicinal benefits which we will be diccussing in the below chapters.

Ajwain Seeds:

The seeds of Ajwain are small and yet are hot and have a penchant and bitter taste. Ajwain seeds possess antibacterial and liver protective properties. In traditional times Ajwain is used for controlling high blood pressure, the active plant enzyme thymol acts as a protective agent. In preparing Indian food ajwain is mostly used in tempering dals. Ajwain gives instant relief from indigestion and acidity problems. Drinking ajwain water clears mucus from the body and gives relief from cough and cold, a regular consumption of ajwain helps in preventing bacterial and fungal infections, it also has antiseptic, antimicrobial and antiparasitic properties which makes it a perfect antidote to infections that cause cough and common cold. Regular consumption can cause benefit's from weight loss, reduced hair fall and glowing of the skin. Many are the benefits and uses of Ajwain which is difficult to mention each and every one. Such is the beauty of Indian spices.

Asafetida (Hing):

Asafetida is the dried latex (oleoresin) extracted from the rhizome or tap root of several species of Ferula, perennial herb growing from 1 to 1.5 meters, they are part of celery family. It's commonly dried and coarsed into small pieces or fine powder. This plant has a bad smell and tastes bitter, it is sometimes called "devil's dung". It is said to have its origin from Rome and despite not being an Indian spice. Asafetida is widely used as a flavoring spice in variety of foods, and commonly used in vegetarian recipes Traditionally it is used for the treatment of various diseases such as asthma, epilepsy, stomach-ache, intestinal parasites, weak digestion and influenza, In India it is commonly known as *hing* it works best for acidity and weight loss. To get a perfect taste of hing to your recipe try to use the original one which is available in the market in the form of small pieces.

Bay Leaves:

Bay leaves also known as (Laurel) is commonly used to flavor soups and non-vegetarian dishes because of its light herbal flavor. There are many species in the bay leaf family all of them share the same taste. It provides Antibacterial, Antioxidants and Antimicrobial protections. Bay leaves are known for their potential ability to protect the body from oxidative stress and from Type2 diabetics. These leaves are rich in the source of Iron, Potassium, Magnesium, Calcium, Vitamin-A, and Vitamin-C, they also help in improving digestive health, treats respiratory conditions. Bay leaf tea is very aromatic and gives relief from sinus and stiffy rose. Generally this leaf is added at the beginning of the dish and while the process of cooking the dish absorbs the aroma, before serving the dish leaf is removed because it is difficult to chew and digest.

Types of Salts:

In India there are 8-10 varieties of salts. I am discussing only *three*varieties of them:

Table salt: This is the most common type of salt and mostly used in kitchens. Sodium Chloride is commonly referred to Table salt, which composition 97% to 99% of Nacl. Salt is a MUST add ingredient to the dish which enhances the taste of the food and also acts as a preservative in food processing. It has also been used in tanning, dyeing, bleaching and in production of pottery and soap industry. During winters suffering from throat infection take a hot water gargle by adding 2- 3 spoons of salt in it.

Black salt: Black salt is often referred to as Himalayan black salt, Indian black salt or Kala namak is a volcanic rock produced in the Himalayan region, it contains Sodium-37mg, Potassium -87mg, Sulphur-450mg, and Iron-43.1mg. The distinct flavor of the salt makes very unique from Table salt. Black salt has low Sodium levels and has Antioxidant properties, It stimulates Bile production in the liver and helps control Heart Burn and Bloating and ease constipation.

Rock Salt: It is also called as Sendha Namak, Simply adding a pinch of Black salt to your Face wash and Body soaps helps in removing dirt, grime and impurities from your skin. Sendha namak is the purest type of salt in India. It is not chemically processed like Table salt does not have iodine hence sold commercially in small quantities being quite expensive. Table salt is crushed into fine structure whereas Sendha namak is in granular form. Sendha is house of vital minerals such as Calcium, Manganese, Iron, Zinc, Potassium, Copper, Sulphur, Hydrogen, and Cobalt. It improves metabolism, maintain body electrolyte balance ensuring normal blood circulation, strengthening bones, muscles. Black salt enhances digestion, sore throat, promotes metabolism, helps to keep the skin clear and also relives stress.

Cardamom:

Elettaria Cardamomum is commonly known as Cardamom, it is a spice made from seeds of several plants. It is known as Elaichi in Hindi. Cardamom is used to build up fat in liver in people who drink little or no alcohol, diabetic and high cholesterol. In food it is used to spice up both sweet and savory dishes, also used in baking cookies, pudding and even cheese cakes, also used in soaps and perfumes. It has many health benefits such as Antioxidant and Diuretic properties and can lower blood pressure. It prevents bad breath, Detoxify the body and removes waste, also helps to fight immune system. This spice is rich in compound called cineole. As a natural therapy cardamom is used for the people who want to quite nicotine chewing cardamom pods 6-8 times a day reduces craving for nicotine.

Cinnamon:

It is called **Dalchini** in Hindi. Cinnamon spice is obtained from the inner barks of several tress from the genius of cinnamonium. It is generally found in sticks form and has a strong Aroma in flavor, generally used in sweet savory and non-vegetarian meals. One of the best way to consume cinnamon is to sprinkle a pinch of it on the food you eat. The chemicals in cinnamon are water soluble and make a great tea. If you want to lose weight especially around your tummy start adding cinnamon to your diet, it suppresses appetite, regulates blood sugar levels, lowers your cholesterol and speeds up your metabolism in addition to torching belly fat. Take cinnamon consistently early morning for life changing benefits. Graciously adding a pinch of cinnamon to your dishes enhances the taste of the dishes.

Cloves:

Cloves are the aromatic flower buds of a tree which belongs to the family of Mytaceae, They are native to the Maluku Islands of Indonesia and are commonly used as a spice, Flavoring, and Fragrance in consumer products such as tooth pastes, soaps and cosmetics. Cloves contain fiber, vitamins and minerals and rich in Antioxidants, so using whole cloves or ground cloves in your food can increase the nutrional value of the food. Clove spice is used mostly used in food such as soups, non-vegetarian foods, preparing sauces, and can also be used as a food preservative. It enhances the flavor of the food. As they are rich in Antioxidants the compound in them helps your body to fight against free radicals present and thereby reduces the risk of developing heart diseases, diabetics and cancer. Cloves are a rich source of beta carotene which helps them retain their brown color, they also helps in reducing the signs of Cirrhosis of liver and fatty liver disease. As said anything taken in adverse is harmful to the body so as clove. Some side effects of cloves can be liver damage and fluid in balancing.

Coriander Seeds:

Coriander is the Herb used annually and belongs to the family of Aplaceae. It is also known as Chinese parsley, Dhania or Cilantro. All parts of the plant is edible, but the fresh stems and green leaves are the parts mostly used in traditional cooking. Coriander leaves and stem has a fragrant, Antibacterial, and Antimicrobial properties. It reduces skin inflammation, controls blood pressure, rich source of calcium controls diabetes, Diuretic properties, (flush out extra sodium from the body) treats mouth ulcers and wounds, and improves digestion. It is the powerhouse of Iron, Vitamin-A and Vitamin-E. Coriander also acts as a remedy for oily skin. Coriander seeds are full of Vitamin-k, which plays an important role in blood clot, it helps your bones repair themselves to prevent from Osteoporosis. Coriander if taken by mouth treats stomach upsets and intestinal problems, nausea, diarrhea. Such are the benefits of coriander seeds.

Cummins:

Cumin is a flowering plant which belongs to the family of Aplacea. Its seeds each one contained within its fruits which is dried and used in many cuisines in many cultures in dry and powdered form. In Hindi it is known as jeera. Research has shown some benefits of Cummins, such as Diabetes, weight loss, cholesterol, Irritable bowel syndrome, stress, and memory loss. Now lets us see some disadvantages of cumin if taken in an adverse proportion. Cummins might lower blood sugar levels and thereby slows blood clotting.

Fennel seeds:

Fennel is a flowering plant which belongs to the family of the carrot family, It is a hard perennial herb with hard feathery leaves, it is especially grown in dry soils and on the banks of riversides, and sea coasts. Fennel plants are highly nutritive and has very good health benefits. In Hindi it is known as (saunf) and used mainly as mouth freshener after lunch and dinner. Fennel in powder or seeds form used in many snack dishes to give a great taste. *India is one of the largest exporter of Fennel seeds.The dried fennel seeds have* various nutrients with low calorific value and high in different micro and macro nutrients, they are rich in vitamin-E, vitamin-K, vitamin-C, Minerals- calcium, magnesium, potassium, Iron, zinc, selenium, Antioxidants such as polyphenol, Fiber and organic compounds such as anethole. It has many health benefits- Combats bad breath, Improves digestion, Helps to regulate blood pressure, Promotes Lactation, Promotes Asthma and other respiratory ailments, Improves skin Appearance, Purifies blood, Keeps cancer at bay, improves eyesight, promotes weight loss, Reduces gasses.

Fenugreek seeds:

This spice is known as *methi* in Hindi. It is an annual plant and belongs to the family of Fabaceae, it's a worldwide cultivated crop leaves and seeds are common ingredients in Indian sub-continent and have been used as a culinary ingredient since ancient times, For thousands of years fenugreek is used as an alternative and Chinese medicine for treating skin conditions and various problems, it has become a common household spice and used in soaps and shampoos. The nutritive value of Fenugreek is -Fiber, Protein, Carbs, Fat, Iron, Magnesium, and Manganese. Other health benefits of fenugreek include-Appetite control, Cholesterol levels, heartburn, Inflammation. Anti cancer effects. It also helps in increasing the testosterone hormone in man, and boots breading feeding in woman.

Curry leaves:

This plant belongs to the family of Rutaceae, and common known as *Kadi patta so sweet neem.* This tree is native to India, and its leaves are used for both medicinal and culinary applications, these leaves are highly aromatic. These leaves are popularly used in cooking dals, rice, and curry and due to its strong aroma added to buttermilk to enhance the taste and flavor. This herb is having health benefits in abundance, curry leaves are rich in Antioxidants they protect your body from oxidative stress and free radicals. Curry leaves are rich in powerful compounds, and may reduce the risk of heart related problems, Neuro protective properties, anti-cancer effects, Pain relieving properties, Antibacterial properties, blood sugar control, curry leaves are versatile and tasty ingredient which can be easily added to wide array of dish.

Dry Ginger:

Dry ginger is nothing but fresh ginger, which has undergone a drying process commonly known as (sonti). In Hindi it is called Adarakh, Dry ginger helps in weight loss by improving digestion, which helps in burning stored fat and processing glucose in the blood. It is easy to digest as compared to fresh ginger, it is bowel binding in nature, dry ginger can be used in all seasons as a spice or as a medicine.

Kalonji:

Kalonji is also known as black cumin is a very popular spice in every kitchen, its a very interesting spice when used for tempering it adds a beautiful aroma to the dish, in India dry roasting of Kalonji is used for flavoring dal, stir-fried vegetables, and even savories such as samosa and kachoris. On the other hand these seeds have a lot of health benefits its loaded with trace elements like vitamins, amino acids, fiber, protein and fatty acids, iron, sodium, potassium, calcium it keeps your heart healthy and lubricates your joints and is known to have Anticarcenogenic properties, increases memory, fights acne, reduces headache, eases joint pains, controls bleed pressure, protects the kidneys, makes teeth strong, strengthens immunity.

Mustard Seeds:

Mustard seeds are small round seeds of various plants. Mustard seeds are commonly known as Sarson in Hindi, All parts of the plant is edible including seeds, leaves, and flowers, they contain minerals like manganese, vitamin-E, Vitamin-C, Vitamin-A, Mustard seeds provide great relief for arthritis they have a strong pungent smell, Health benefits of mustard seeds reduces migraine, cancer treatment, cancer risk prevention, Respiratory congestion, hydrating the skin to slow down ageing signs, may increase cardiovascular health, and increasing appetite.

Nutmeg:

Nutmeg is the spice made from the seed of the nutmeg tree (Myristica Fragrant), Nutmeg is rich in fiber and keeps digestive system healthy, and prevents blood sugar from increasing. Its also rich in vitamin-A, vitamin-C, vitamin-E, Zinc, Magnesium, Manganese, Nutmeg tastes warm,nutty, and sweet.Nutmeg is rich in Antioxidants, including phenolic compounds, essential oils and plant pigments, all of which prevents celluar damage and protects aganist from chronic diseases. This spice has a variety of uses in kitchen, it can be used alone or can be spiced alond with cinamom, cardamon, or cloves. It has a sweet flavor due to which is added in deserts and sweet dishes, cakes, cookies etc.,Nutmeg can cause serious side effects like rapid heart attack, vomiting, nausea, and even death. when consumed in large or mixing with other recreational drugs. Try to enjoy this spice very carefully as there is a risk for life.

Black Pepper:

Black pepper is a flowering vine piperaceae cultivated for its fruit peppercorn which is usually dried and used as a spice, It is the native to the malabar coast of India and is one of the earliest spice known.Black pepper is very spicy spice and is found in every kitchen used more oftenly in form of powder or as whole. It is called *king of spices. Black* pepper is rich in potent antioxidant called piperine which may help prevent free radical damage to your body. It may promote Gut health, pain relief, reduce appetite and boosts in absorptions of nutrients. It is a versatile spice having many Ayurvedic properties.

Star Anise

Star anise are evergreen fast growing tress that occasionally grow upto 26 feet ,used as a spice and source of pharmacutical chemicals. Its named for the star shaped pods from which the spice seeds are harvested and has a flovor that is reminiscent to licorice. Star anise is rich in variety of flavonoids and polyphenolic compounds. It is used in medicine for treating bacterial, fungal, and viral infections. Star anise has a distinct flavor for which it is used in stews, deserts, broth, soups, and baked foods.

Saffron:

Saffron is the spice derived from the flower Crocus Sativus commonly known as Saffron. It is very powerful spice with antioxidants, It has health benefits such as sexual function, libido, improved mood, Golden colored pungent stigma is dried and used as a spice to foods and as a dye to color foods and other products, Saffron has strong excotic aroma and bitter taste. Saffron has 0.5- 1 %essential oil. **It is the most expensive spice in the world. The dye has** been used for Royal garments in various cultures. The streets of Rome are sprinkled with saffron when Nero entered the city.

Turmeric:

Turmeric powder is bright yellow color spice powder, made from dried turmeric Rhizomes. It has slightly peppery and warm flovor with bright yellow color, It is often seen as a star ingredients in beauty treatments due to its antibacterial, antifungal properties and antioxidant rich nature. Consuming turmeric by mouth seems to reduce hay fever symptoms such as cough, sneezing,itching, running nose and congestion. worried about sleepless nights, then graciously add a pinch of turmeric powder in a glass of luke warm milk, and let the magic begin.

Red chilli :

In India they are different varities of chillies, to name some of them Red chillies, Green chillies, Gntur chillies, Kashmiri chillies, Dangi mirch and many more. All these are categorised depending upon there intensity of spiceness, texture, and color, Indian food is famous for its blend in spice, and masalas. Chilli peppers are widely used in many cuisines to add spice, and heat to the dishes, Chilli pepper has preventive and therapautic properties for many ailments such as different types of cancer, Rheumatism, Stiffness of joints, bronchitis, cough.cold and headache.

Poppy seeds:

Poppy seeds are the seeds from poppy plant. Poppy seed is a oilseed obtained from oplum poppy, it is widely used in many countries, poppy seed oil is used to make soaps, paint, and varnish. These seeds are often used for various benefits promoting digestionm boosting skin and hair,treating headaches, cough and asthama.poppy seeds are good source of dietary fibre,as well as some essantial vitamins and minerals including calcium and magnesium, theyare used widely for culinary purposes.

CHAPTER II

How to prepare Masalas in your kitchen

A blend of fragrant Indian spices in dry or paste form It is used to flavor many traditional foods and beverages throughout the region. Several different varieties of mixture exists, each one is having its own unique spice blend, taste and flavor. This blend often features pepper, clove, star anise, cummin,Dhania seeds, and many more spices,This vividly intense seasoning is used in junction with other spices or alone in various dishes. Many chefs prefer to make their own freshly blends instead going for readymade as this gives more taste to the dish served.

Dhania powder/ Coriander powder

This powder is very easy to prepare, and hardly takes much time. For making 250grms of Dhania powder below are the listed ingredients.

Ingredients: Dhania/ coriander seeds-250grms
Preparation: It is a simple 3 step process
Step-1

- Take a heavy bottomed pan, keep your flame on medium, allow the pan to heat completely. Now add the coriander seeds in batches (250gms), Reduce the flame to low and stir the ingredients continously not to get burn untill the aroma of coriander seeds is released switch off the flame and tranfer all the ingredients to a clean plate(see that the plate is completely dry) to stop the process of further roasting. Allow the coriander seeds to cool for upto 15-20min. When cooled transfer the ingredients to the food processor/a mixie jar.

Step-2

- After transfering the ingredients to the jar, Grind the seeds on pulse in between open the lid and clean the surroundings of the jar so that the mixtures dosent stick to the edges of ths jar, Repeat the same process untill it becomes to a fine powder.

Step-3

- Now transfer the powder to the sieve and sieve it thoroughly, make sure there are no grannules left if you find some please again transfer the grannules to a jar and repeat the process once again. Your home made coriander powder is ready to use. Dont forget to store the powder in a clean glass container, while going through the process dont enjoy the awesome aroma of the powder, surely it motivates you to prepare again and again and keep you at bay to purchase the ready made one.

Chat Masala Powder

Chat masala powder is generally used for sprinkling on all street food dishes like Aloo chat, Bhelpuri, Dahipuri, Pani puri and many other such dishes. generously sprinkling this powder along with few drops of lemon does a magic to Salads, and fresh fruits because of its Zesty taste. Let us look at the ingredients needed to prepare this masala.

Ingredients:
1/4 cup- cumin seeds,
2 tbsp coriander seeds,

2- inch dry ginger,
2-no's dried Red chilli,
2tbsp- Black pepper,
1/2 spoon- cloves,
1/2 netmug,
3 tbsp -dry mint,
1/4 cup- dry mango powder/ dried pomogrante seeds,
Hing, and salt as per taste.
preparation:

- **To** start with take a heavy bottomed pan, add 1/4 cupof cumin and 2tablespoon of coriander seeds,
- dry roast the spices on a low flame till the aroma is released.
- Now transfer the roasted spices to large plate and make sure to cool completely.
- In the same pan add dry ginger, Dried Red chilli, Black pepper, cloves, and nutmeg,
- Reduce the flamr to medium and dry roast carefully so that spices may not burn
- Roast till the spices release their aroma.
- transfer all the ingredients to a plate, and allow to cool
- In the same you can dry roast mint leaves/ or you can use sun dried mint leaves
- transfer to the same plate and allow to cool
- Now transfer all the dry roasted spices to the mixie jar
- add mango powder, hing, and salt as per taste
- Blend to fine powder, make sure all the ingredients are blended properly
- Finally home made chat masala is ready to use on your Aloo chat or any food of your choice

Yes, please dont forget to store the powder in a clean air tight container.

Rasam powder:

Ingredients:
75 gms- coriander seeds,
25 gms - cumin seeds ,
20 gms - methi seeds,
few curry leaves,
100 gms-Dried Red chilli,
hing, salt, turmeric.
Preparation:

- **Take a** heavy bottom pan, Add coriander seeds, cumin seeds, methi seeds, and dried red chiili
- Put the flame to low and dry roast all the spices
- till they release the aroma, take care spices should not burn.
- transfer all the ingredients to a plate
- and cool them
- now on to the same pan add curry leaves, and dry roast untill all te moisture gets absorbed and leaves turn crispy in texture.
- allow curry leaves to cool
- transfer all the spices to a mixie jar
- add salt, turmeric,hing,
- Grind all the spices to a fine powder
- store in a clean air tight container
- The shelf life of Rasam powder is comparatively more than other masala powder

You can prepare in large quantity and refrigerate for the same taste and aroma.

Red chilli Powder (For regular use)

Red chilli powder is an authentic spice, which is a must in your spice box, Being a versatile spice it is used in preparing many dishes. the main ingredients used here are very handy and available in your kitchen, Raw chilli powder can't be used for daily, because it harms your stomach and may lead to acidity and ulcers in the stomach. while preparing this chilli powder various other spices are used while preparing this chilli powder, on the other it enhances the taste of the dishes. I would call it "**All in one multi purpose masala**"

Ingredients: For making 250gms of chilli powder

250 gms of Red chilli,

please remove the stems and see that the Red chillies are of good quality depending on the color of your chillies the texture of your masala depends.

10- no.s Garlic pods,

1/2 cup- coriander seeds,

2 tps- cumin and mustard seeds,

1/2 tps- fenugreek seeds,

salt as per taste,

1 tsp -oil.

Preparation:

- Take a wide pan add 250 gms of red chilli to the pan, please note - always keep the flame to low while roasting the chillies,
- *now add 1 tsp of oil to the red chillies to avoid over roasting of chillies,
- transfer the roasted chillies to a plate, allow to cool
- in the same pan add coriander seeds, cumin, mustard, fenugreek seeds
- and roast them till they release the aroma
- tranfer the spices to a plate, and allow to cool them completely
- Tranfer all the spices including red chillies to a mixie jar
- add garlic pods and salt to your taste
- Now grind all the ingredients to make a fine powder
- your all purpose chilli masala powder is ready to use
- use it generously to enhance the taste of your dishes.

Dont forget to store in airtight container.

Garam Masala Powder

No wonder garam masala is popular all over the world! It is easly available in small and big stores across all over the world in indian shopes. Depending upon the region spices may differ, but the basic recipe will be the same, This recipe will make you understand how to prepare garam masala.Every cuisine has a special ingredient which gives it a charateristic flavor and aroma. for example if you consider south- Indian food it is sambar powder, when comes to Noth-India it is garam masala takes over in this way according to the region the flavour changes. It is nothing but a blend of variety of spices.

Ingredients:

To start with- 1/2 cup- cuminns (jeera)

- 1/2 cup-cardamom (choti elaichi)
- 1/4 cup- black pepper
- 2 cups- coriander seeds/ dhania
- 3tps- fennel seeds(saunf)
- 2tps- cloves
- 5 small sticks-cinnamon(dalchini)
- 3 - bay leaves(tejpatta)
- 1/2tps- shah jeera
- 1/4 tsp.- nutmeg powder
- 2 no's- star anise
- 2 no's Badi elaichi

preparation:

- **Take a** wide pan, heat the pan in a low, medium flame and ensure that there is no moist in the pan
- Now add all the above spices to the pan, slowly stir dry roast all the ingredients in a low

- When the spices release the aroma while roasting, consider it done.
- Transfer all the ingredients to a big plate, to stop the process of roasting and allow it to cool completely.
- now add all the roasted spices to a Maxie jar,
- and grind them to a fine powder
- Sieve the powder and discard the left over powder, or you can grind once again for a smooth powder.
- Garam masala powder is ready to use, as it is said its uses are very versatile you can use it preparing biryani, dry/ wet curries, masala curry or according to your taste
- Please don't forget to store in a air tight container this increases it shelf life and help to maintain the magic aroma to stay intact.

Sambar Powder

Sambar powder is a south Indian style flavoured spicess powder, prepared by blending various types of Indian spices like black pepper, cloves, cummin, coriander, cinnnamon, dry red chillies, coconut, and some pulses, along with a magic ingredient Hing, sambar powder is incomplete without Hing and curry leaves.

Ingredients:
1/4 cup- chana dal
1/4 cup- urad dal
1 cup- coriander seeds
2 tsp- black pepper
1 tsp- cloves
1 tsp- jeera
1 tsp - Fennel seeds
1/4 tsp- methi seeds
1 cup- dry coconut
2 strands- curry leaves
Hing
2-3 - cinnamon sticks

Preparation:

- Take a heavy a heavy bottomed kadai, heat the kadai on a low flame
- Add chana dal and urad dal to the kadai, and dry roast by continously stirring to avoid over roasting and burning of the puleses.
- Now transfer all the pulses to a plate and allow it to cool
- Now to the same kadai add all the ingredients except coconut powder and red chillies
- A sthe above procedure dry roast the spices till they release the aroma
- Transfer the roasted ingredients to the plate and let them cool
- In the same kadai add red chillies, curry leaves,
- Roast continously till done
- Transfer all the ingredients to a plate
- switch off the stove, and in the same kadai add coconut powder and roast till the dampness is reduced.
- Transfer all the roasted spices along with pulses to a mixie jar , and grind till all the things are done to a fine powder
- now add coconut powder and a small crystals of hing and grind finely
- *Hing is the magic ingredient here, and adds to the flavour, aroma, and taste of the dish
- Before storing it to a container make sure that it is dried out completely, without any moisture.
- your sambar masala is ready to use,
- This masala can be used in some of your stir fry vegetables. to rasam , to add taste to the dish.

please don't to enjoy the aroma of the spices while preparing after that gives a fealing of happy cooking like satisfaction in the END!!

Gun powder

Gun powder or Kandi podi is the Andhra style chutney powder recipe, Generally it is served with ghee or til oil. I preferably don't know why its called Gun powder may be due to the spiceness/ heat generated because of red chillies (while preparing gun powder try to use Guntur chillies for a kick start spiceness. There are many variates of this chutney podi/ gun podi , out of which one recipe i am sharing with you all.

Ingredients:

1 cup- chana dal(bengal gram)

1 cup - Roasted chana dal

10 pieces - dry Red chillies (depending on the how much spice you would like to have)

10 - pod's - garlic

1-tsp cummin seeds

5 - strands of curry leaves

salt as per taste

one small lemon size- tamarind

Asafoetida

preparation:

- In a wide open pan , first dry roast chana dal with continously stirring
- Remove the dal to a plate and allow to dry
- In the same pan add rest of the ingredients cummin seeds, curry leaves, Red chillies, and roast them till you can smell the aroma of the spices
- Now transfer all the ingredients to the plate and allow to cool
- After cooling combine all the pulses and roasted spices to the mixie jar and grind to make fine powder
- open the lid of the jar and clean the edges, now add tamarind salt, hing , garlic pods, and salt
- finally blend together to form a fine powder, taste the podi to adjust the salt

- your home made podi is ready to serve with Idlis, Dosa or with Hot steamed Rice along with ghee adds wonder's to the taste.
- you can store the podi and use it whenever there is a short of curry for lunch or dinner.

*Take Away Bonus Masala

Shahi Chicken Masala

A really special Shahi garam masala powder which can be added to non-vegetarian dishes and also to biryanis, dum biryanis and at times to curries. This gives a very strong taste and aroma.

It is a perfect proportions of all the aromatics, which gives a unique flavour to the dish.It is a perfect combination for mutton dum biryani. This perfect home made shahi chicken masala takes your dish to a next level. * This masala is very strong so you need to just add one oe two spoon full to get that punch to your dish. TRY to buy the fresh spices and use it immediately. you get a perfect masala. Now let us see what are the ingredients needed to make this masala that much special.

Ingredients:
1 cup- coriander seeds
1/2 cup- fennel seeds
3-4 -sticks of cinnamon
1/2 cup- cummin seeds
10- big bay leaves
10 pieces- green cardamom
5- star anise
10- black pepper
5- cloves
procedure:

- Take a wide mouth pan, make sure the flame is in medium low

- Add all the spices to the pan, and stir continously till the aroma of the spices is released
- now transfer all the ingredients to a big plate , and cool them for 10-15 min
- Take a mixie jar and add the spices to the jar
- blend them to a fine powder
- cool the powder
- store in fridge and add to your dishes as per requirement.
- shelf is more for this masala powder so no need to worry.

CHAPTER III

Important tips to follow while preparing and storing

- Make sure the ingredients are roasted well, to remove the moist present in them
- If you are grinding your masalas at home make sure the mixier grinder is completely dry, or you can use a piece of cloth to remove the dampness of the jar.
- Spread the masalas on the newspaper and let them dry completely, because while the process of grinding the spices become hot, and need to be completely dries before storing in an container.
- For retaining the freshness and aroma of the masalas they need to be stored in the refridgerator and use as per needed.
- Try to use fresh spice formaking masalas and not the stored ones.
- To increase the shelf life of the masalas don't open the containner with wet hands, wet spoons, or spatula, always used moist free spoons whenever required
- If you are not keeping in the fridge the use glass jars to store the spicess.
- Sun dry the containner before using.